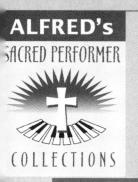

ALFRED's
SACRED PERFORMER
COLLECTIONS

What Can I Play for ...?

MW00784122

10 Easily Prepared Piano Arrangements

Arranged by Cindy Berry

Through the years, I have been privileged to play the piano for many weddings. Often, I have had to use several different sources to find the songs that I wanted to include. As an addition to the *What Can I Play on Sunday?* series, this collection contains every type of arrangement that a pianist might need when playing for a wedding. Included are some pieces that can be used for the processional (both for the wedding party and the bridal entrances), and a couple of pieces that are traditionally played for the recessional. There are also arrangements, both classical pieces and hymns, that can be played for the prelude time or for the lighting of a unity candle. Approximate performance times for each piece are included to assist in planning. I hope that this collection will be useful to you as you help brides and grooms celebrate their special day!

Cindy Berry

Alfred Music Publishing Co., Inc.
P.O. Box 10003
Van Nuys, CA 91410-0003
alfred.com

ISBN-10: 0-7390-7109-2
ISBN-13: 978-0-7390-7109-0

BRIDAL CHORUS

Richard Wagner
Arr. Cindy Berry

With majesty ($\quad$ = ca. 76)

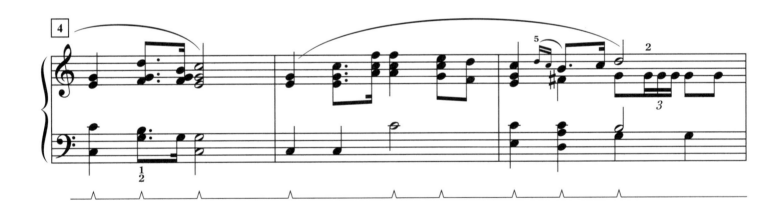

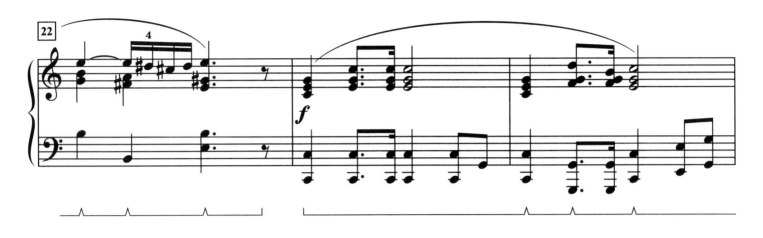

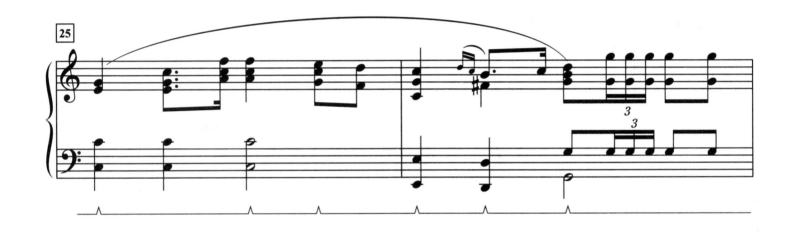

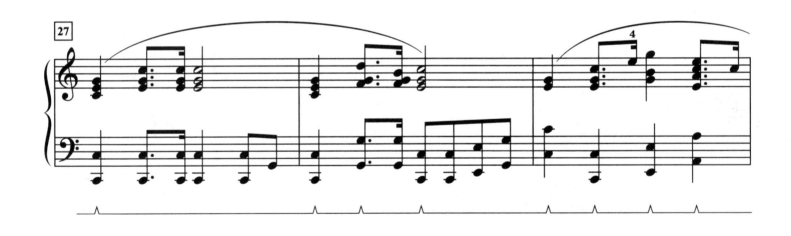

(Approx. Performance Time – 2:15)

Canon in D

Johann Pachelbel
Arr. Cindy Berry

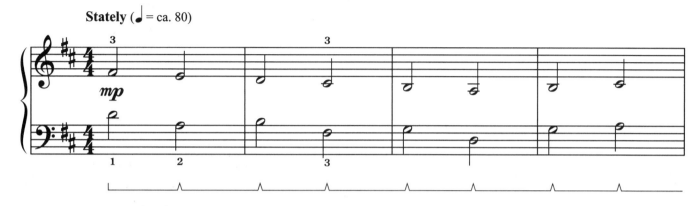

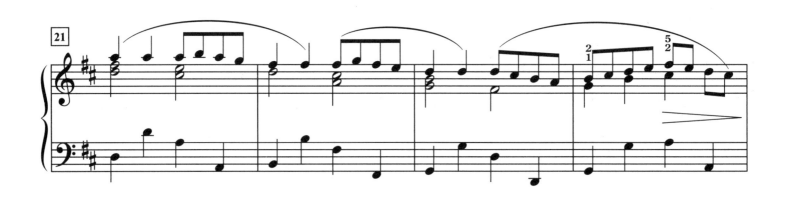

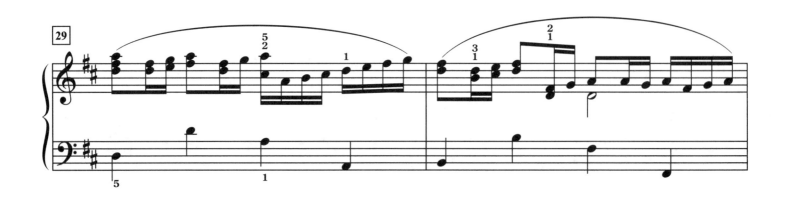

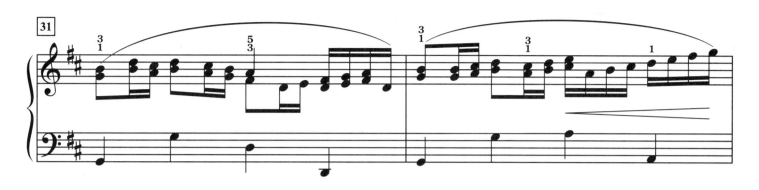

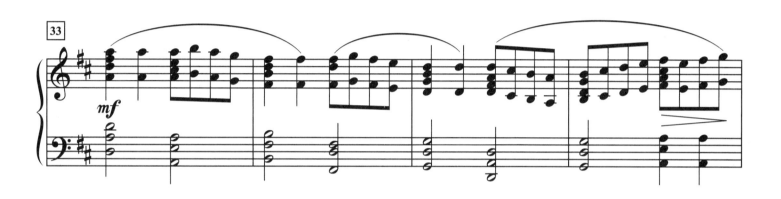

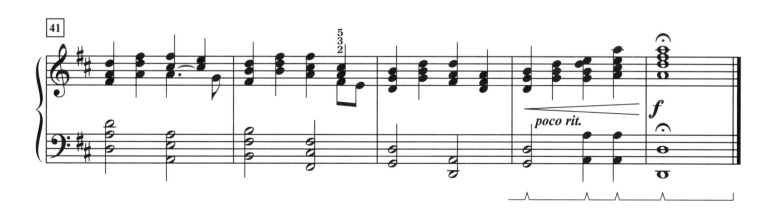

(Approx. Performance Time – 2:45)

HOLY, HOLY, HOLY

John B. Dykes
Arr. Cindy Berry

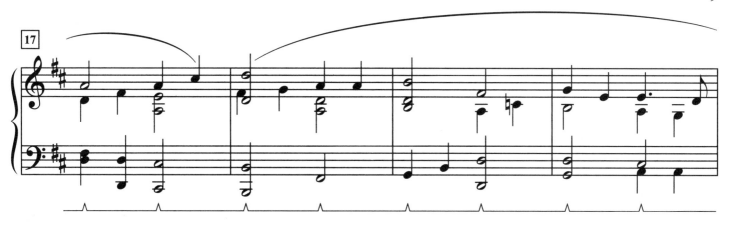

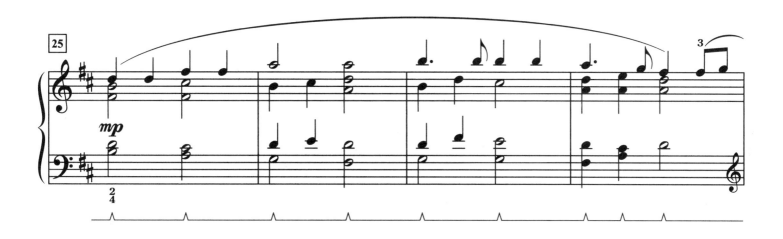

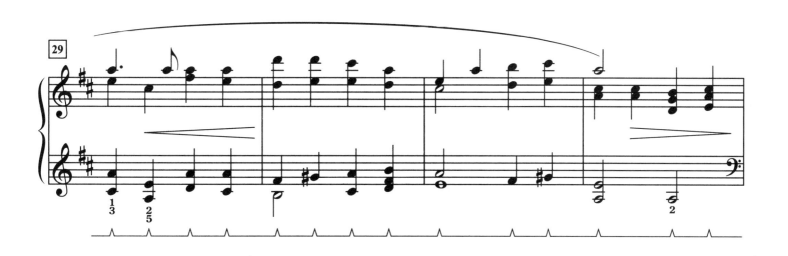

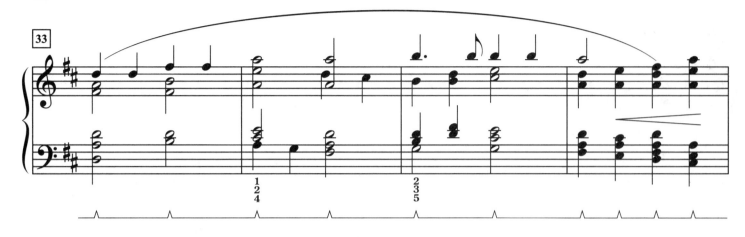

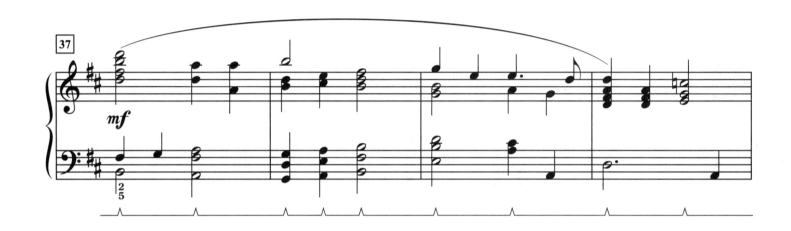

A little slower (♩ = ca. 80)

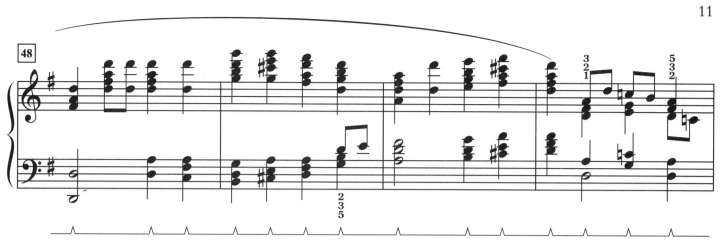

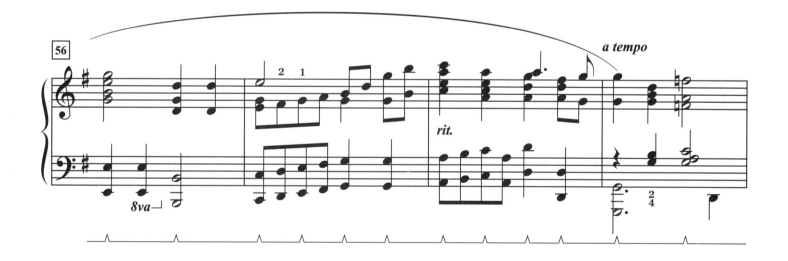

(Approx. Performance Time – 2:00)

Air (from Water Music)

George Frideric Handel
Arr. Cindy Berry

(Approx. Performance Time – 3:45)

PANIS ANGELICUS

Cesar Franck
Arr. Cindy Berry

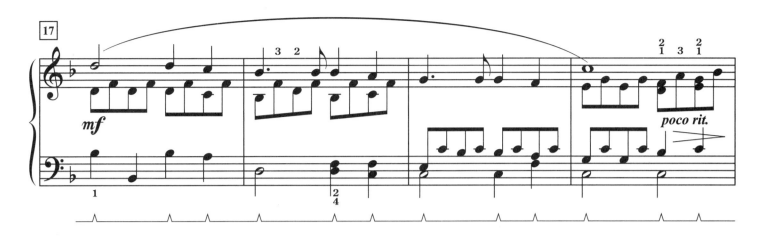

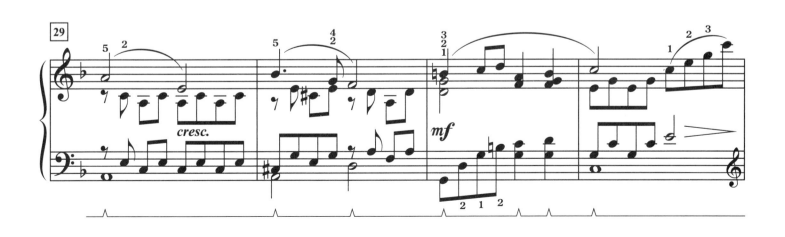

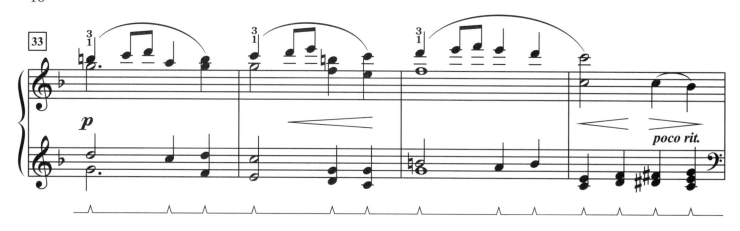

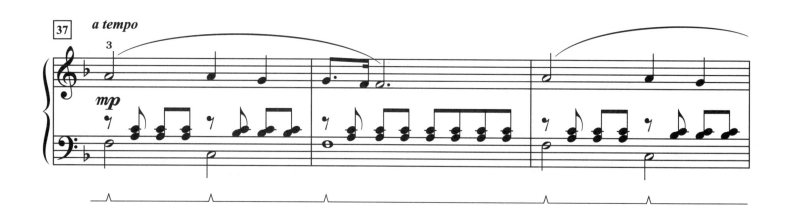

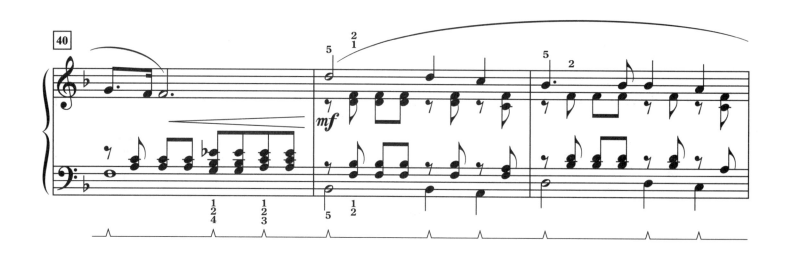

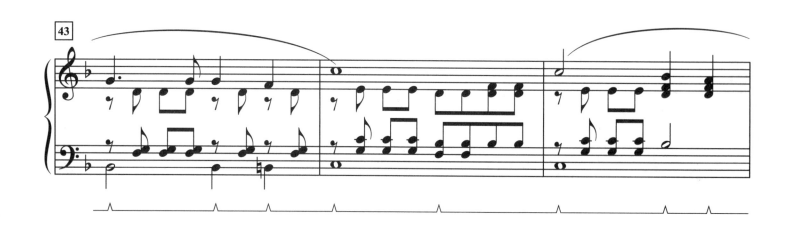

(Approx. Performance Time – 3:15)

ARIOSO (FROM CANTATA NO. 156)

Johann Sebastian Bach
Arr. Cindy Berry

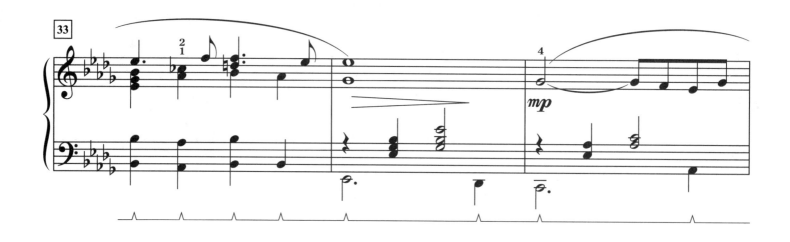

Savior, Like a Shepherd Lead Us

William Bradbury
Arr. Cindy Berry

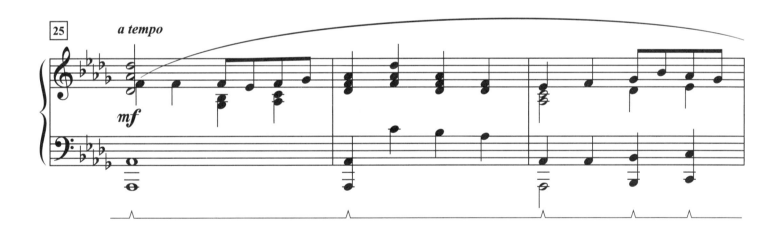

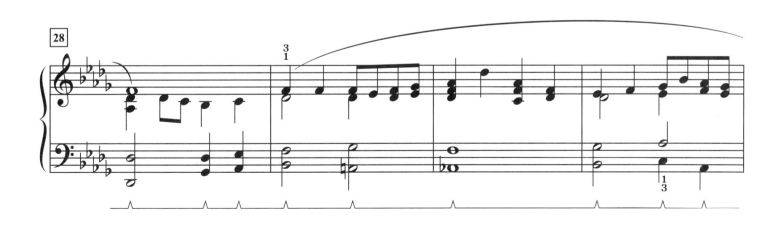

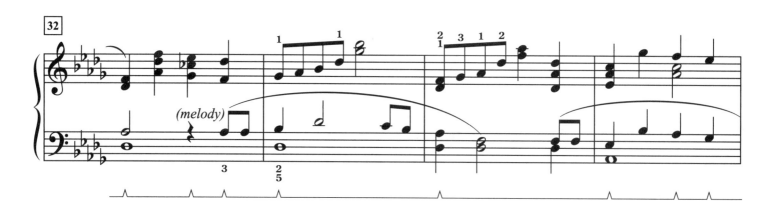

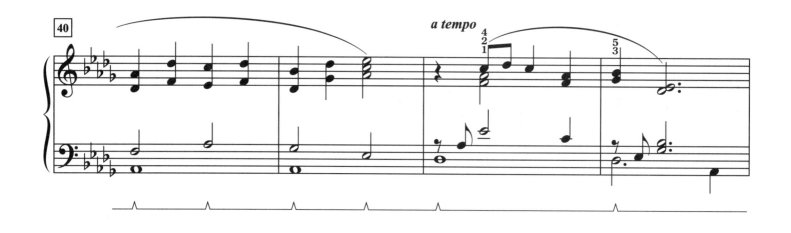

(Approx. Performance Time – 2:30)

BE THOU MY VISION

Irish Folk Melody
Arr. Cindy Berry

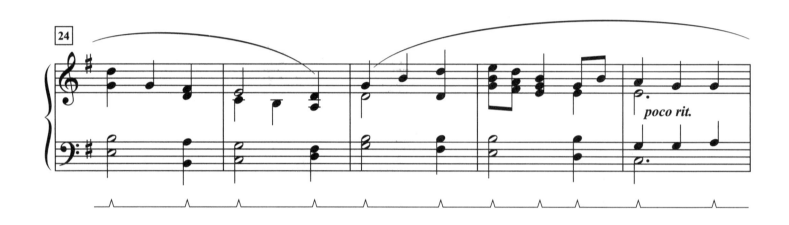

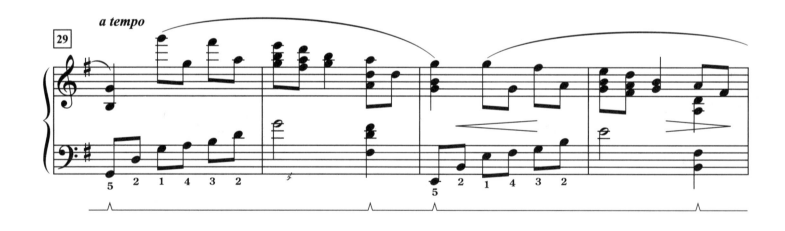

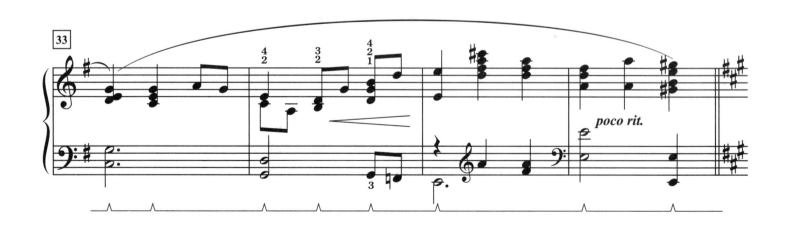

Psalm 19

Benedetto Marcello
Arr. Cindy Berry

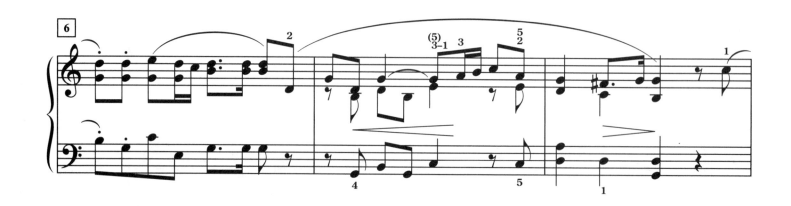

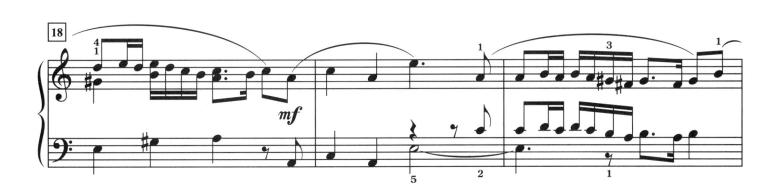

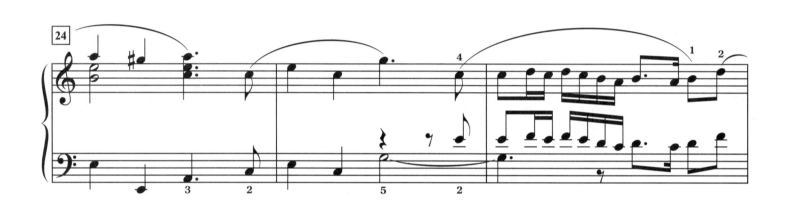

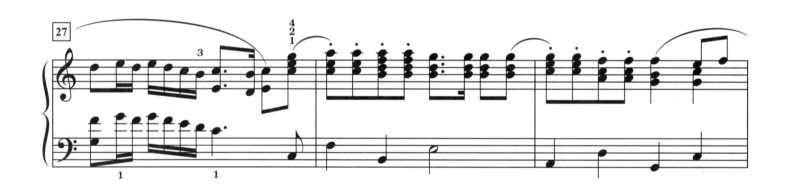

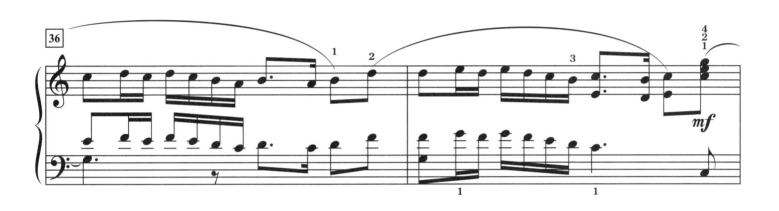

(Approx. Performance Time – 1:45)

WEDDING MARCH

Felix Mendelssohn
Arr. Cindy Berry

Joyfully (♩ = ca. 126)

(Additional ending—optional)*

*If optional ending is used, disregard the *rit.* in measure 40.